Quito, E[cuador]
TOWNSCAPE
WALKS

S. Domingo
plaza

12 Routes
- cafes
- plazas
- museums
- churches
- monuments
- neighbor hoods

inca
stones

Walk
with Me Tyler
Burgess

Published by:
Walk with Me
1430 Willamette St. #579
Eugene, OR 97401 USA
Printed in Quito, Ecuador

These are unique routes I
designed as I walked them.
As we all know, Shift happens.
Construction changes and
business turnovers alter the
area. Updates are welcome.

Global Mapping Software
was used for base maps.

Thank you to my son,
Damon Cole, and his
girlfriend, Susana Vega,
for their hospitality
and assistance.

Townscape Walks books
 by Tyler Burgess
• Siena, Italy
• Seattle, Washington
• Portland, Oregon
• Oregon, 22 towns
• Eugene, Oregon

Walk-With-Me.com

What is a Townscape Walk?

"For a city is a dramatic event in the environment."
George Cullen, "Townscape" 1961.

What makes a walk dramatic?
"The Line of Life" Why is this city here?
Walks start in the historic center, then into neighborhoods. Visit museums along the route to learn history.

fruit market

"Grandiose Vista": It links you, in the foreground, to the remote landscape, thus producing a sense of power, or omnipresence. Dr. Suess expressed it as,
"I'm Yertle the Turtle!
Oh Marvelous Me! For I am ruler of all that I see!"

"Mystery of the Emerging View":
What is around the corner, over the hill, down the path?

"The Silhouette": With a curve, a steeple, the buildings soar up to catch the sky, netting it as the butterfly net catches its prey.

"Seeing in Detail": A window, a symbol, an arch, a bridge, fences.

Outdoor rooms, porches, and benches create seclusion or invite social activity.

quotes from "Townscape" by George Cullen, 1961

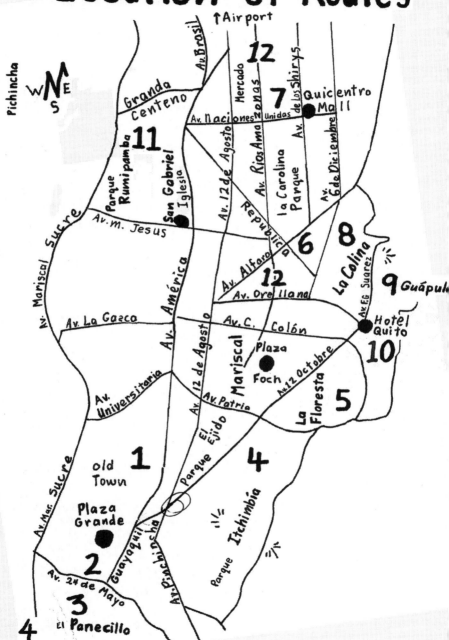

Table of Contents

Page

Directions to the start.   7

Routes

1. Plaza Grande to La Basílica   8
   2 mi. or 2.5 mi. 282 ft. elevation gain
   •Centro de Arte Contemporáneo
   • Casa de Sucre • La Catedral de Quito
   (home of)

2. Plaza Grande to Calle La Ronda   10
   1.7 miles, 220 ft. elevation gain
   •Centro Cultura Museos (Museums)
   • San Francisco Iglesia (church), Museo

3. Plaza Grande to El Panecillo, with taxi
   2.5 mi., 287 ft. elevation gain   12
   4.8 mi. 575 ft. elevation gain
   •San Roque Iglesia • San Diego Convento

4. La Mariscal to Parque Itchimbia   14
   1.3 mi. flat. 3.2 mi. 50 ft. up
   5.3 mi. 575 ft. up.
   •Museo Nacional del Banco Central

5. La Mariscal to La Floresta   16
   2.5 mi. 111 ft. up
   •Museo de Artesanías Mindalae

6. La Mariscal to Parque La Carolina   18
   2.5 mi., 4 mi. or 4.6 mi. all flat
   • Jardín Botánico (Botanical Garden)
   •Corfu and Cyrano-ice cream, sweets

7. Quicentro to Mercado Tradicional **20**
2.3 mi. 50 ft. up

8. Quicentro to La Colina **22**
2.5 mi., 3 mi., or 5.2 mi. 220 ft. up.
• Jardín Botánico (Botanical Garden)

9. La Colina to Guápulo **24**
1 mi. 475 ft. down, taxi up.
2 mi, or 2.7 mi. 475 ft. up
• Guápulo Iglesia, Museo (church, museum)

10. La Colina to La Floresta **26**
1.5 mi. 50 ft. up.   2 mi. 110 ft. up

11. San Gabriel to Rumipamba **28**
2 miles, 310 ft. up. 4.75 mi. 600 ft. up
• Rumipamba Archeological Park

12. Avenue Río Amazonas **30**
About 5 miles are closed to auto traffic every Sunday. Beautiful!
• Events in the parks.

About the author and illustrator **32**

Legend

● Start and finish here
••• shorter option
🗻 hill

RR Public restrom, 10¢
ft. up = elevation gain

mi. = Mileage

R turn Right

L turn Left ✋

→ to #(7) indicates connecting route

How to get to the start:

Taxis are recommended, as they are cheap and plentiful. Cost is no more than #3.00, plus a few cents tip.
Before starting, look to see if the meter is set to 50¢.

The Metro Bus is 25¢. See the tourist map for lines.

Plaza Foch is Plaza El Quinde on some maps.

Longer routes:

Several routes connect, plus several share a common start.

Start and connecting points:

Start Point	Route	Connects to
1. Plaza Grande	to La Basílica	2, 3, 4
2. Plaza Grande	to Calle La Ronde	1, 3
3. Plaza Grande	to El Panecillo	1, 2
4. Mariscal Pl. Foch	to Itchimbía	1, 5, 6
5. Mariscal Pl. Foch	to La Floresta	4, 6, 10
6. Mariscal Pl. Foch	to Parque la Carolina	4, 5, 7, 8
7. Quicentro Mall	to Mercado	6, 8, 11
8. Quicentro Mall	to La Colina	7, 9, 10
9. Hotel Quito	to Guápulo	8, 10
10. Hotel Quito	to La Floresta	8, 9
11. San Gabriel Iglesia	to Rumipamba	7
12. Av. Río Amazonas	— whole length	1 to 8

Plaza Grande to La Basílica

Distances: <u>2 miles</u>, 173 ft. up.
<u>2.5 miles</u>, 287ft. up.*

Start/finish: Plaza Grande in Old Town.
·Restrooms are under arches
along Chile street, in Centro
Comercial, in Patio de Comidas, 10¢.

Stand at the lowest part of Plaza
Grande, facing uphill.
R on Venezuela street.
Visit La Basílica.   *(Return for 2mile option.)
Continue on Venezuela.
Curve **L** up to big, white Centro
de Arte. Visit for #2, restrooms.
R after exiting. Cross street.
Up stairs, then up stairs to park.
L on first path, to end.
R up stairs to path. **R** past statue,
to end. Stay on main path.
L on street, Benalcázar.
R on Galápagos, 1 block.
L on Cuenca, 1 block.
L on Esmeraldas, down stairs.
Cross Benalcázar, go **R**.

Flag
of the
Revolution

R on Mejia, 1 block.
L on Cuenca, to steps to big plaza.
L on Sucre, at these steps.
R on Venezuela, go 50 steps to
Casa de Sucre, on **R**.
Visit for #1, restrooms.
Exit, **L** to La Catedral de Quito, #1.50.
Exit from same entry,
L on Venezuela to Plaza Grande.

Fresh
Juice

Almacén
Yepez at
5-23 Sucre

8

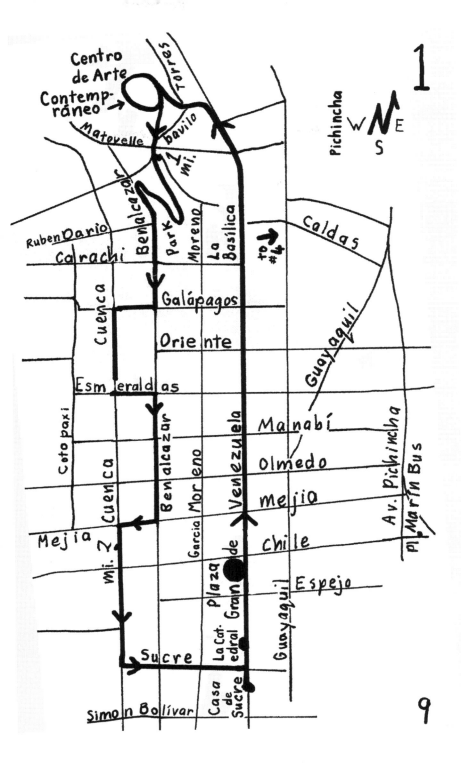

Plaza Grande to Calle La Ronda

Distance: 1.7 miles, 220 ft. up.

Start/finish: Plaza Grande in Old Town.
     •Restrooms are under arches along
         Chile, in Centro Comercial
         in Patio de Comidas, 10¢.

Face the Palace, be in front of
the Palace, at the top, highest
part of Plaza Grande.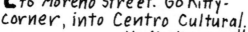
L to Moreno street. Go Kitty-
corner, into Centro Cultural.

     Visit the small, free museums in
         the salas. Continue through the
         interior arches. Exit **L**.
         Cross street (Moreno). Visit Iglesia
         de la Compañía de Jesús.

Continue on Moreno, 1 block.
R on Sucre. Veer **L** in big
plaza. Up steps to visit the
San Francisco museo and
  Iglesia. #2.

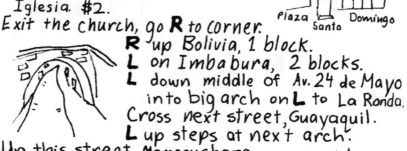

Plaza Santo   Domingo

Exit the church, go **R** to corner.
    R up Bolivia, 1 block.
    L on Imbabura, 2 blocks.
    L down middle of Av. 24 de Mayo
        into big arch on **L** to La Ronda.
    Cross next street, Guayaquil.
    L up steps at next arch.
Up this street, Mamacuchara.
Across Santa Domingo Plaza.
R on street along plaza, Guayaquil.
L up Sucre, 2 blocks. **R** on Moreno.

2

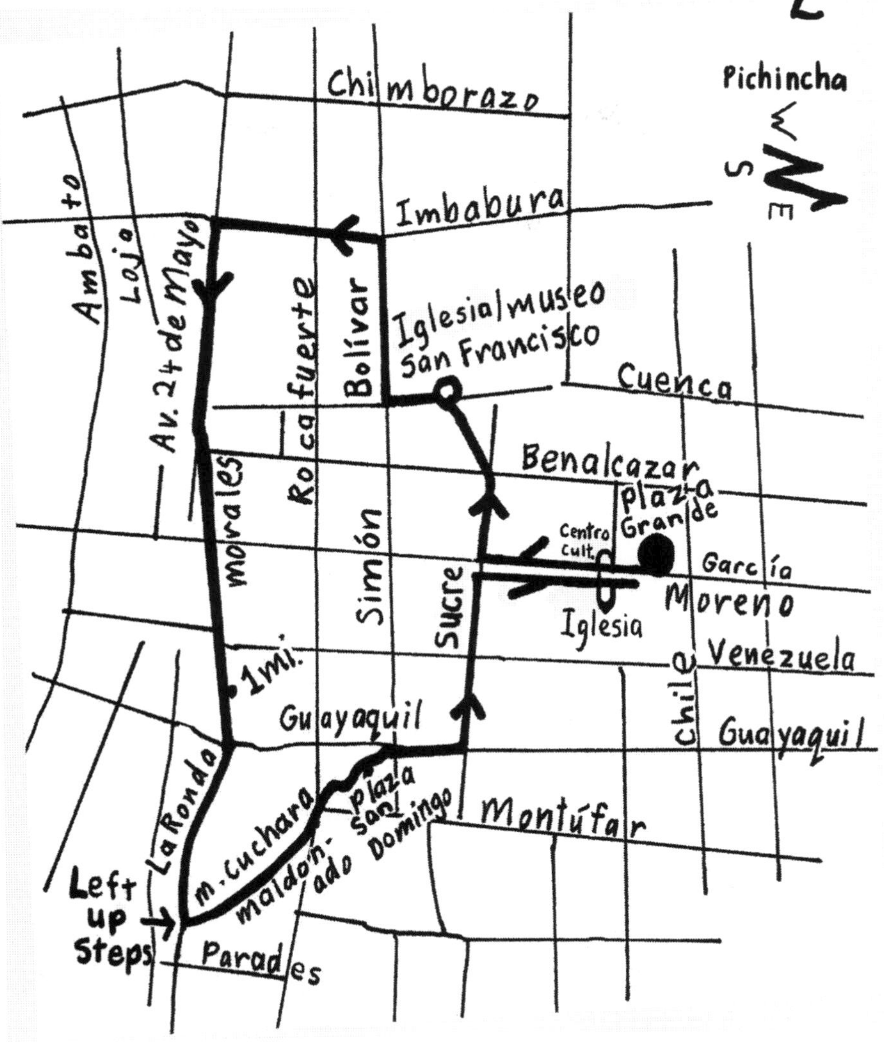
Pichincha
W
N
S
E
Chimborazo
Imbabura
Ambato
Lojo
Av. 24 de Mayo
Rocafuerte
Bolívar
Iglesia/museo
San Francisco
Cuenca
Benalcazar
plaza
Grande
Centro
Cult.
García
Moreno
Iglesia
morales
Simón
Sucre
Chile
Venezuela
1mi.
Guayaquil
Guayaquil
La Ronda
m. Cuchara
plaza
San
Domingo
maldon-
ado
Montúfar
Left
up
Steps
Parades

Plaza Grande to El Panecillo

Distances: <u>2.5 miles</u>, 287ft. up, plus taxi.
<u>4.8 miles</u>, 575 ft. up, plus taxi.

Start/finish: Plaza Grande in Old Town.

Face the Palace, at the top, at highest part of Plaza Grande.
•Restrooms are under the arches, on Chile, in Centro Comercial, in Patio de Comidas.

R to Chile, **L** up Chile.
L on Chimborazo.
R on Rocafuerte.
Visit San Roque church.

L on Cumandá. **L** on Loja.
Up the covered steps, over.
R on Imbabura, through plaza.
Veer **R** at 5 way intersection.
Go into cemetery, go straight.
•Restroom **L** of entrance, or nicer ones inside, past church.
•Please, No photos, No talking.
R at end, 1 block. **R** at church.
Exit cemetery, go **L** (Imbabura.)
(Visit San Diego church, if open).

L at end, La Ermita/Farfán, 1 block.
L on Cestaris. Cross bridge, go **L**.
Straight to sidewalk with handrail.

fruit market

(for 2.5 miles) — Take a taxi from here to El Panecillo, about $1, and back to Plaza Grande.

(for 4.8 miles) — Follow sidewalk with handrail up to el Panecillo. Return to busy street, Caraquez. Take a taxi to Plaza Grande, $1.30. Do NOT walk back.

Pichincha

W N E S

Mejia Lequerica

Chile

Plaza Grande

Espejo

mideras

Imbabura

Chimborazo

Alianza

de Benalzar

Moreno

Venezuela

Guayaquil

Simón Bolívar

Cuenca

V. Rocafuerte

Sab.

Garcia

Cumanda

Loja

Ambato

Ab. Calderón

Imbabura

Barahama

Do not walk back

Quiñonez

La Ermita

San Diego convent

Ba. Caraquez

G. W. Aymerick

3 mi.

2 mi.

get a taxi back from here.

Farfán

cemetery

can get a taxi to top.

4 mi.

Gral.

Celstaris

Panecillo

La Mariscal to Parque Itchimbía

Distances: <u>1.3 miles</u>, flat. To Centro de Arte and back.
<u>3.2 mi.</u> 50 ft. up to Parque Alameda and back.
<u>5.3 miles</u>, 345 ft. up.

start/finish: Plaza at Mariscal Foch and Reina Victoria
With your back to the big sculpture,
face Reina Victoria St. **R** on R. Victoria.
At end, **L** to corner, **R** across street.
R along park and Patria street.
L through arch, into Parque El Ejido.
(1.3 mi.=**L** to Museo del Banco Central.)
R on path, **R** to pass the red flame.
At park end, continue straight,
along Av. 10 de Agosto . at sign.
L up stairs at N14A. Cross street, Borja, go **R**.
Up tower in park. **L** on park path, Alameda park
R across 2 bridges. **R** at round building and
R after building. Take path on **R**. (3.2 mi=return
At end, **R** on crosswalk. **L** to corner.
R up Briceno. **L** on Vargas, 1 blk.
L on Caldas, 1 blk. **R** on Guayaquil.
L on first crosswalk, cross plaza.
Up steps. (Restrooms at SSHH).
L on Los Rios. Curves **R** onto Castro. 2 blocks.
R on Iquique, into Parque Itchimbía.
After entrance, **R** to grass path. Stay on path
as it circles the park. At the end, tour the
cultural center. Exit down steps, back to Iquique
L on Solano, Cross Llona, go **L**.
R on Yaguachi. **R** on Colombia.
At Solano, cross Colombia, continue.
L on Medio. Straight at roundabout,
emerging on Patria. **R** onto Leonidas.
L at end, on Foch. At Av. 6 Diciembre,
L to use crosswalk. Continue on Foch.

14

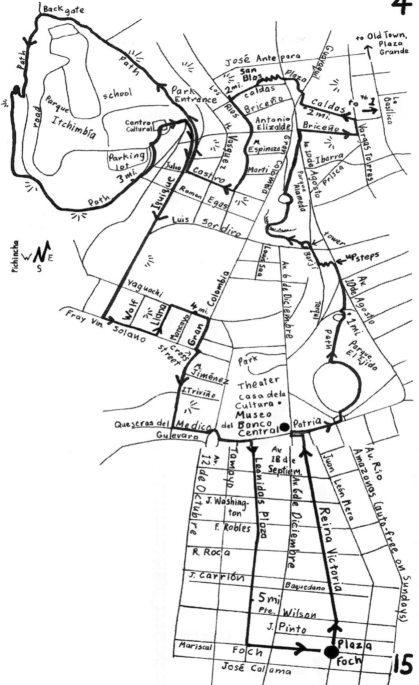

La Mariscal to La Floresta

Distance: 2.5 miles, 111 ft. up

Start/finish: Plaza Foch at M. Foch and Reina Victoria.
With your back to the big sculpture, face Reina Victoria St.
L on Reina Victoria.
R on La Niña.
L at end, ½ block.
At first crosswalk, cross street.
L for ½ block.

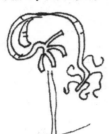

Museo de Artesanía Mindalae at La Niña $3.00

R up Orellana street, 2 blk. **R** on La Colina.
L up San Ignacio, ½ block.
R on Caameño.
Cross next street, Colón.
Jog **R** then **L** on Destruge.
L on Salazar, 3 blocks.
R on Valladolid (no sign), 1 block after Toledo.
After OCHOYMEDIO, continue downhill to next corner.
R on Galavis.
L on Andalucia, 1 block.
R on Galacia.
L on La Católica.

Dios Le Pague Cafe
OCHOYMEDIO
Disfrutti Té

famous and delicious tea

R on Caameño, which becomes Veintimilla after 12 de Octubre.
R on Reina Victoria to Plaza.

5

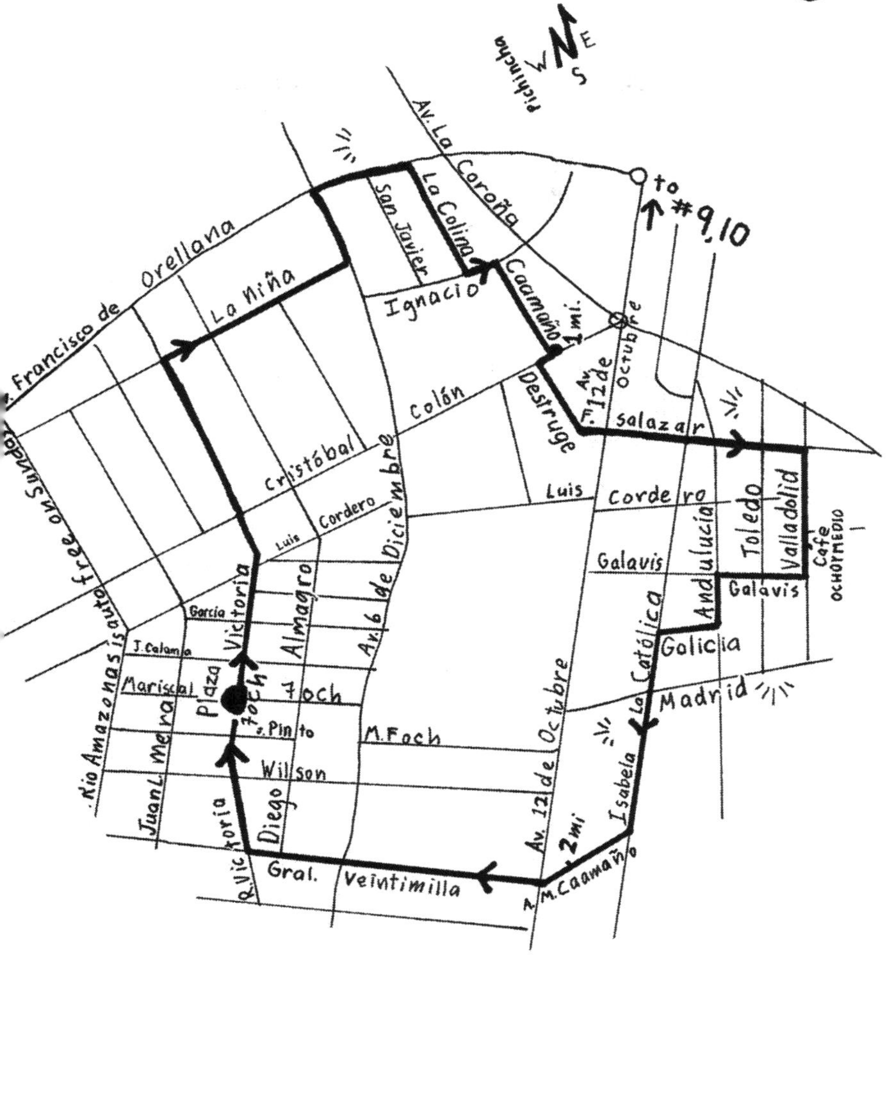

Pichincha
N
W
E
S
Av. La Coroña
to
#9,10
Francisco de Orellana
La Niña
San Javier
La Colina
Ignacio
Caamaño
1 mi.
Av. 12 de Octubre
F. Destruge
Salazar
Colón
Cristóbal
Av. 6 de Diciembre
Luis Cordero
Luis Cordero
Galavis
Galavis
Toledo
Valladolid
Andalucía
Cafe Ochomedio
free on Sundays
Rio Amazonas is auto
García
Victoria
Almagro
J. Calama
Mariscal
Plaza Foch
Foch
Juan L. Mera
Golicia
La Católica
Isabela
Madrid
Av. 12 de Octubre
P. Pinto
M. Foch
Wilson
Diego
R. Victoria
2 mi
Gral. Veintimilla
A. M. Caamaño

La Mariscal to Parque La Carolina

Distances: <u>2.5 mi.</u> to Park and back.
             ❋<u>4 mi.</u> to Corfu for ice cream,
                   coffee, pastries; and back.
             <u>4.6 mi.</u> All flat route.

Start/finish: Plaza at Foch and Reina Victoria.

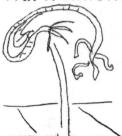

With your back to the big
sculpture, cross R. Victoria st.
Go 1 block on Foch.
L on Almagro. (Restrooms
   at corner of Moreno.)
Curve **L**, stay on Almagro.
Cross Orellana, veer **R**.

L on Aguilera, before busy street.
R at end, on Pradera.
Cross Republica, go **L**.
Take crosswalk into the park.
Go to big, brick statue.
R on main path to circle ⟶
the park.

❋ Corfu and Cyrano Detour:
Just before the second
parking lot in the park, look
R for crosswalk to Portugal
street. go ½ block, the shops
are on the left.

25 roses
$1.00

When you arrive **back** at the big,
brick statue, go **R** to corner,
go on República (left-side).
R at cross walk onto Pradera.
L on Aguilera, **R** on Almagro.
R on Foch.

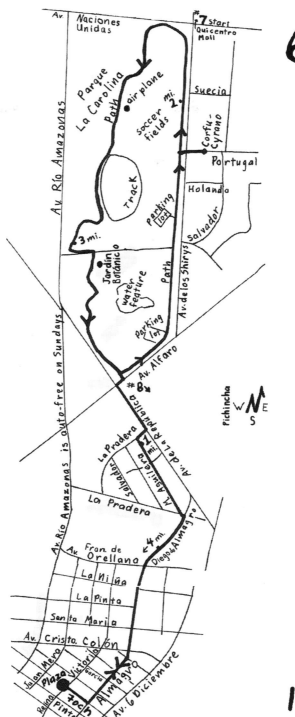

6

Quicentro to Mercado Tradiciónal

Distance: 2.3 miles. 50 ft. easy uphill.

Start/finish: Quicentro Mall, main entrance.
Cross Av. de Los Shyris.
Go straight on *Naciones*, 1 block.
Walk next to shops, not street.

Roasted Pig

R on Japón. **L** on A. Guerrero.
R on M. Ayora.
L on V. Cardenas. 1 block.
L on Av. Río Amazonas, 1 block.
R on Pereira, 1 block.

Mercado
es Tradición
ancestral

"La Carolina"

L into the Mercado. (Restrooms
  are near this entrance,
  outside the Mercado.)
Exit the same door you entered.
Continue around the
outside of the Mercado to the
far corner.

R on J.J. Villalenaua.
R on 10 de Agosto. Go up stairs,
over bridge, and straight
to corner.
Cross Diguja, go **L** 1 block.

creation

In the Beginning
was the word.

L on Veracruz, 1 block.
L on J.J. Villalengua.
Over the same bridge.
Stay on J.J. Villalengua.
R on Av. Río Amazonas.
L on Av. Naciones Unidas, walk
  along store fronts.

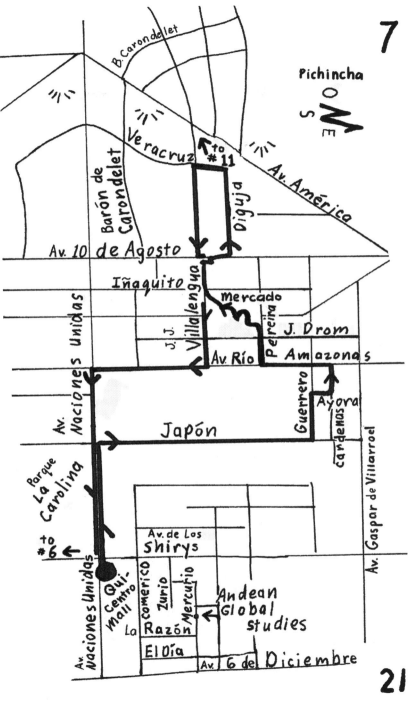

Quicentro Mall to LaColina

Distances: <u>3 miles</u>, flat. See ✳ and →below
               <u>5.2 miles</u>, 220 ft. up.
Start/finish: Quicentro Mall, main entrance.
               R on Av. Naciones Unidas, ½ block.
               L over bridge. **L** 100 ft. to pond.
               R on main path. (Restrooms 10¢).
When you see the greenhouse,
L on path, **R** along greenhouse.
(Straight to visit Botanical Garden).
Continue straight after fence.
Path curves **L**. At this big,
brick sculpture, **R** off main
path.

Cross street at light, Alfaro. Go **L**.
R on Tobar. **R** at end, on park
path. **L** on Alpallana.
Veer **L** on Whimper.
At 6 Diciembre, **R** across Whimper.
✳ (for 3.5 mi. **L** on Alamagro. **L** on Shirys. See →below)
L to cross Diciembre.
Up Whimper.

green house

Stone wall is
earthquake proof
N31 -129 Humbolt

L on Coruña, 1 block. **L** up steps.
Cross street. **L** on upper Coruna.
Curve **R** on Humbolt, ½ block.
L up steps. **L** on upper Humbolt.
R on Gomez. **L** on Gonnessiat.
R on Bejarno. **R** at next street, Suárez.

cool cafe with wc

la liebre

After Nescafe sign, cross Suárez.
R to La Liebre Cafe. Return on Suárez.
R through roundabout. Curves **L**.
R over bridge. At bridge end, cross street.
Up steps. **L** one block.   —careful—
L on Bossano. At light, cross street, go **L**.

mosque

R at next light, Av. de Los Shyris.
→ Cross Av. Gral. Eloy Alfaro into park.
R on bike path, past sidewalk. Curves **L**.
R to cross bridge. **R** along shops

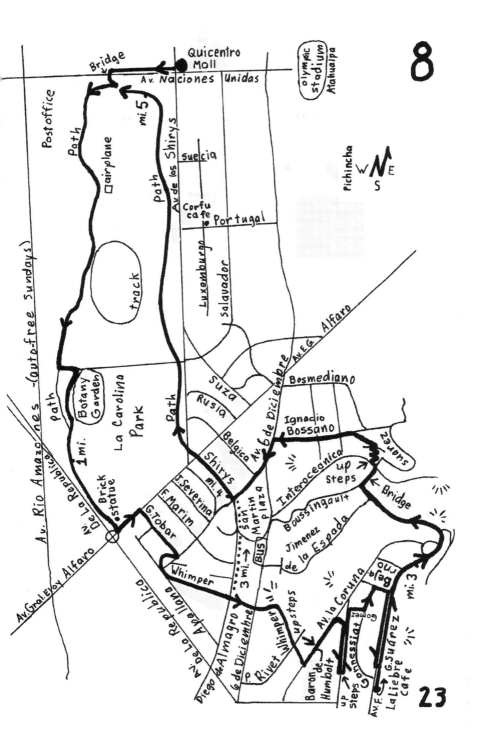

La Colina to Guápulo

Distances: 1 mile, 475 ft. down. Take a taxi up.
Taxi stand is across from church.
2 miles, 475 ft. down, less steep up.
2.7 mi. 530 ft. down, less steep up.

start/finish: Hotel Quito, on Av. F. Suarez, N27-142.
Face the street. Go **R** 2 blocks.
R on R. Leon Larrea. After viewing
platform, go 100 ft.
L through gate into park.
Follow path to street.
L at street, through passage.
R down stairs.

R at street, Fray F. Comte.
L at corner onto Toro. Make
R turns until in front of church.
Visit. Museum hours: M-F 9-12, 3-5 $1.50
Continue around the church.

(2mi.= **L** up El Calvaro.
Cross street, stay on path.
L at street. Join at ✱ below.)
Straight down Compte.

Loops back up on Camino Orellana.
✱Straight at intersection at Larrea.
R up steps where shops begin.
R on street, Mirabella, 1 block.
Turn onto Zaldumbide.

Curves **R** onto Av. Isabel La Catolica.
R at US Embassy to view.
Curve **L** onto Av. F. de Orellana.
R at corner Plaza Abe Lincoln,
on to Av. F. Gonzales Suarez.

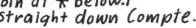

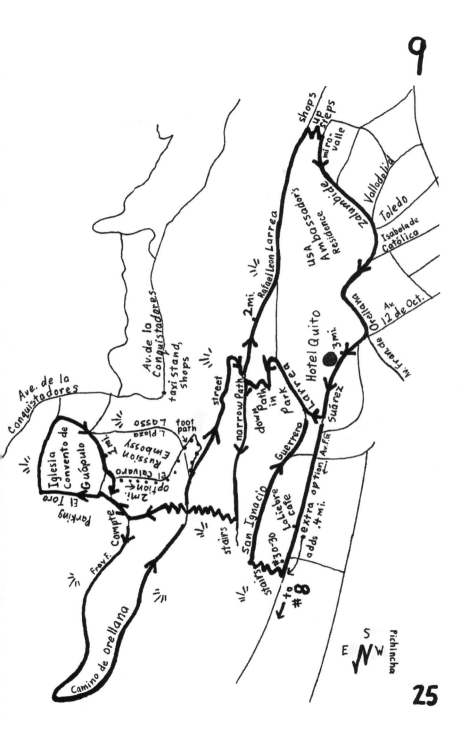

La Colina to La Floresta

Distances: .6 mile 50 ft. up. ⎫
1.5 miles 60 ft. up. ⎬ down stairs,
2.1 miles 110 ft. up ⎭ easy up.

start/finish: Hotel Quito, N47-142 Av. Suárez

cool cafe
½ block past stairs

la liebre
video cafe
II •WC
on Suárez

Face the street. **R** to building
Torres de Guápulo No. 30-30.
After the building, **R** down
stairs.(or ½ block to La Liebre)
R on street, Ignacio, Curves **R**.
✷(Continue up to end. **L** on Suárez.)

L on Guerrero.
L down Rafael Leon Larrea,
Curves **R**. where shops
begin, **R** up stairs.
✷(1.5 mi.= **R** at top, Miravalle.
Curves **L**. **R** at each corner.)

Cafe
Dios le Paque
Disfrutti Té

L at top, on Miravalle.
Curves **R** on Rubio de Arevalo.
R on Valladolid, 1 short block.
L on Toledo, 2 blocks.
L on Salazar, 1 block.
R on Valladolid, 1½ blocks to
  Dios le Paque cafe, cinema

famous and
delicious tea

www.OCHOYMEDIO.net

From the cafe, return on Valladolid, ½ block.
L on Cordero, 2 blocks.
R on Andalucia, 2 blocks.
Jog **L** on Salazar, **R** on Católica.
At end, cross street, go **L**,
on Av. Orellana, 1 block.
R at Plaza Abraham Lincoln,
on Av. 12 de Octubre.

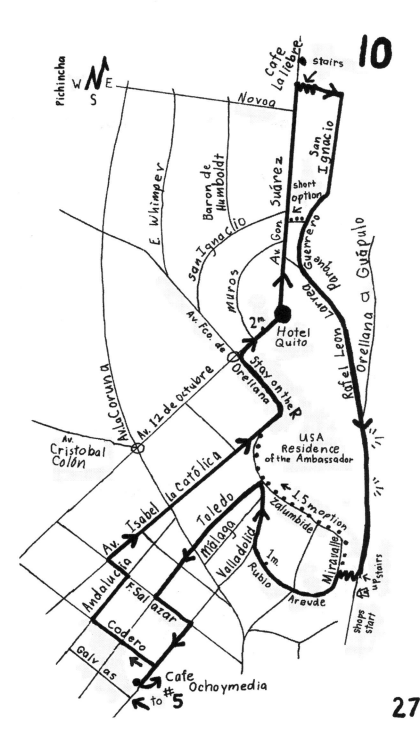

San Gabriel a Rumipamba

Distancias:

Un jarrón de una tumba antigua

3.2 km. 95 m. elevacion de San Gabriel Iglesia.
Sube la Av. M. de Jesus. **D** antes del túnel, a Rumipamba Arqueología Parque. Vaya * abajo. Regrese a la iglesia.

7.5 Km. 185 m. elevacion

Inicio/final:

San Gabriel Iglesia en Av. M. de Jesus.
Camine de cuesta para abajo en Av. M. de Jesus.
I en América. **I** en Rumipamba, 2 cuad.
D en Vasco de Contreras, al final.
I en A. Granda Centeno, al final
I en Miranda, al final, en Mañosca.

D en Mañosca, al final.   **O** tome una taxi a Parque Rumipamba
D sube el puente.
Camine derecho por una cuadra.
Sube las escaleras a la iglesia amarilla.
Ande alrededor y vuelva la calle.
Continúe en la misma dirección.

I baje del túnel. Cruce la calle primera. **I** al Parque Rumipamba.
* **D** baje de calle en el parque a la oficina. Consigue una guía y visite el parque, 1 hora Vuelva a calle y vaya **I**.

Despúes el Hospital de la Policia.
D en N. Arteta y Calisto, al final.
I en San Gabriel, 3 cuadras.
I en N. de Valderrama.
Cruce Av. Jesus vaya **D** baja della colina, 60 metros.

evacaviones

I en el Parque República. (SSHH baños)
Tome el camino principal hacia abaja.
Sala del parque. Continúe abaja de la cuesta.

28

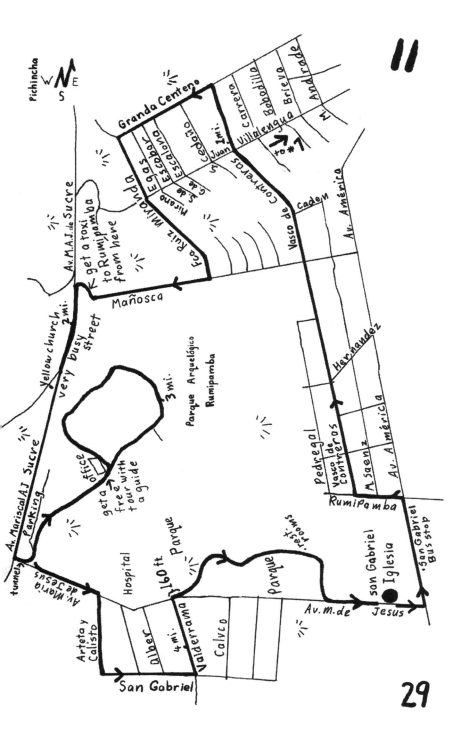

Avenue Río Amazonas

Distance: about 5 miles one way.

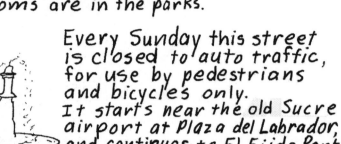

Start and finish anywhere along the Av. Río Amazonás. Restrooms are in the parks. (10¢)

Every Sunday this street is closed to auto traffic, for use by pedestrians and bicycles only.
It starts near the old Sucre airport at Plaza del Labrador, and continues to El Ejido Park. You can continue to Plaza Grande.

Free events in the parks, with music, food, markets. Do this walk only on a Sunday, as it is too busy other days.

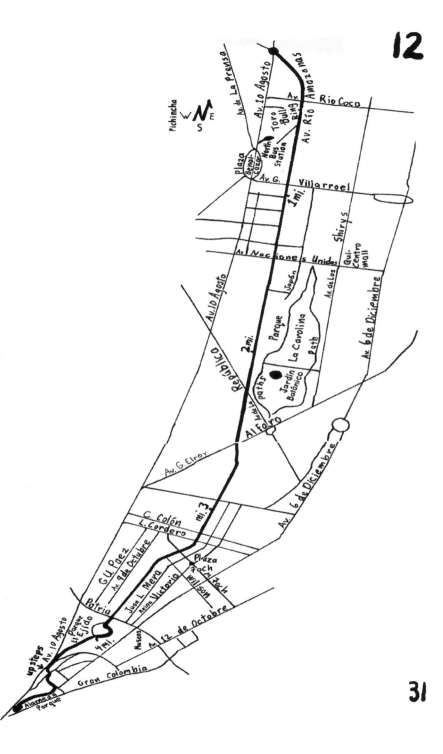

About the Author and Illustrator, Tyler E. Burgess

Born in 1950 in the shadow of the Bighorn mountains, I grew up on a cattle ranch near Sheridan, Wyoming. While earning a Business degree at the University of Wyoming. I married, had two children, Sara and Damon. We moved to Billings, Montana, raised the children, divorced and eventually I moved to Eugene, Oregon, where my son was a student.

For athletics, I have always loved outdoor sports. In my 40's I played soccer, did triathlons, multi-sport events, solo backpack trips.

In 2000 I founded Walk With Me, and have coached marathon walking training, taught fitness walking classes at the University of Oregon and Lane Community College.

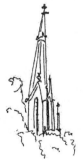

Also I have organized and led walking trips across England, in Ireland, Italy and Morocco. Plus New York City, Boston and Washington DC.

In the fall of 2008 I did a solo walk 550 miles in Spain, the pilgrimage, Way of St. James.

Made in the USA
Las Vegas, NV
10 October 2021